Spirituality
of the Psalms

FACETS

Spirituality
of the Psalms

Walter Brueggemann

Fortress Press
Minneapolis

Contents

Preface

The Psalms are a strange literature to study. They appear to be straightforward and obvious. They are not obscure, technical, or complicated. Yet, when one leaves off study of them, one is aware that the unresolved fascination endures. Any comment upon them is inevitably partial and provisional. That is certainly true of such a limited manuscript as this. The reason for the partial, provisional character of this study is not simply because of such limitations, but because of the nature of the material. There is simply more than can be touched and handled. So one finishes with a sense of inadequacy, of not probing enough. That, of course, is why the Psalms continue to nourish and nurture long after our interpretation has run its course. We are aware that the claims of the literature have not been exhausted.

1. I have assumed the great deposit of critical scholarship that is indispensable for study of the Psalms. I have not thought it useful or necessary to repeat all of that, or even to specify the sources I have drawn upon. But it will be evident that I am dependent on and do take seriously that fund of critical learning. Indeed, my basic plan of organization is derived from the form-critical consensus.

2. I have utilized a "scheme" of orientation – disorientation – new orientation. But I want to say, both to those who may critically assess this book and to those who may use the book as a door to psalmic spirituality, that I do not intend the proposed scheme to be a straitjacket. I do not imagine that the scheme is adequate to comprehend the Psalms, for we do not have such a "master key." I intend this principle of organization only to help us see things we might not have seen otherwise. The test of a good paradigm is whether it serves in a heuristic way for future study. Most specifically I have used this device as a way of showing how the "psalms of negativity" may be understood in the life of faith.

3. In an attempt to be "postcritical," I have had in mind especially the pastoral use of the Psalms. By that I mean how the Psalms may function as voices of faith in the actual life of the believing community. So I have sought to consider the interface between the flow of the Psalms and the dynamics of our common life. I am cautious, if not suspicious,

about any neat grid of developmental stages or "passages." I am equally cautious about any neat grid of the Psalms, but it does seem clear that there are moves and seasons in the life of faith, even if we encounter them in various ways. I have sought for the interface between *those experiences common to us* and *the offer of faith* in the Psalms. I do not want to be rigid about this or reductionist. But I want to show that such a pastoral agenda can benefit from critical scholarship and need be neither excessively popular nor obscurantist.

Of the critical methods available, I have largely followed the form analysis of Gunkel, refined in important ways by Westermann. The threefold scheme I have used is centrally informed by the genre of the Psalms. Second, I have been surprised to find that Mowinckel's understanding of the creativity of the cult has been more helpful than I had expected. It has been mediated to me through Peter Berger and Thomas Luckmann and their understanding that the "social construction of reality" is an active, creative task. The cult — organized, communal worship (or wherever such social construction happens) — is a setting for imaginative, creative speech that forms new worlds for us. And this is not remote from our experience. I have also tried to pay attention to the emerging methods of sociological and rhetorical analysis that are latent in Gunkel's work but only now coming to full attention. These methods suggest, as I intend to show, that what goes

on in the Psalms is peculiarly in touch with what
goes on in our life.

4. I have felt no obligation fully to cover all of
the Psalms. If the scheme has viability, it may suggest how other psalms might also be placed and
understood in relation to the whole. Specifically I
have not paid attention to the royal psalms, the
songs of Zion, or to the great historical recitals.
They did not strike me as the most useful for the
present work. But that does not mean they are without value for pastoral concerns.

5. My main interest has been theological. I have
concluded at the end of the study (and not as a presupposition) that the shape and dynamic of the
Psalms can most usefully be understood according
to the theological framework of crucifixion and resurrection. By that I do not want to turn the Psalms
into a "Christian book," for I have repeatedly
stressed the profoundly Israelite character of the
material. Rather, I mean the following:

(a) The moves of orientation – disorientation –
new orientation are for Christians most clearly
played out in the life of Jesus of Nazareth, but not
exclusively there. I find Philippians 2:5-11 a helpful
articulation of this movement. It can, without any
forcing, be correlated:

Orientation: "Though he was in the form of God . . ."
Disorientation: "[He] emptied himself."
New Orientation: "Therefore, God has highly exalted
him. . . ."

The Gospels, and especially the passion narratives portray his life in precisely that fashion, perhaps with special affinity to the liturgical destiny of the king.

(b) The liturgical form of this same matter is, for the life of the church, evidenced in baptism. The same two moves that I have sketched in the Psalms are the key discernment of baptism:

> We were buried therefore with him by baptism into death . . . that as Christ was raised from the dead . . . we too might walk in newness of life. (Romans 6:4)

We understand in baptism that the loss of control of our lives (disorientation) is the necessary precondition of new life (new orientation).

(c) In the radical reflection of the Old Testament (in Jeremiah, Ezekiel, and Second Isaiah) these same moves are made around the destiny of Jerusalem. It is a city that must be plucked up and broken down in order that it may be built and planted (Jeremiah 1:10). That same sense of deep cost and discontinuity has been important for Jews in trying to understand the Holocaust and the surprise of the state of Israel.

(d) All three dimensions of our tradition, the life of Jesus, the baptism of Christian believers, and the destiny of Judah's fortunes around Jerusalem, attest to the reality that deep loss and amazing gift are held together in a powerful tension.

The gain in this for the study of the Psalms is that it shows how the psalms of negativity, the complaints of various kinds, the cries for vengeance and profound penitence are foundational to a life of faith in this particular God. Much Christian piety and spirituality is romantic and unreal in its positiveness. As children of the Enlightenment, we have censored and selected around the voice of darkness and disorientation, seeking to go from strength to strength, from victory to victory. But such a way not only ignores the Psalms; it is a lie in terms of our experience. Brevard S. Childs is no doubt right in seeing that the Psalms as a canonical book is finally an act of hope. But the hope is rooted precisely in the midst of loss and darkness, where God is surprisingly present. The Jewish reality of exile, the Christian confession of crucifixion and cross, the honest recognition that there is an untamed darkness in our life that must be embraced – all of that is fundamental to the gift of new life.

(e) The Psalms are profoundly subversive of the dominant culture, which wants to deny and cover over the darkness we are called to enter. Personally we shun negativity. Publicly we deny the failure of our attempts to exercise control. The last desperate effort at control through nuclear weapons is a stark admission of our failure to control. But through its propaganda and the ideology of consumerism, our society goes its way in pretense. Against all of this the Psalms issue a mighty protest and invite us into a more honest facing of the darkness. The reason the darkness may be faced and lived in is that even in the darkness, there is One to address. The One to address is in the darkness but is not simply a part of the darkness (John 1:1-5). Because this One has promised to be in the darkness with us, we find the darkness strangely transformed, not by the power of easy light, but by the power of relentless solidarity. Out of the "fear not" of that One spoken in the darkness, we are marvelously given new life, we know not how. The Psalms are a boundary (Jeremiah 5:22) thrown up against self-deception. They do not permit us to ignore and deny the darkness, personally or publicly, for that is where new life is given, whether on the third day or by some other uncontrolled schedule at work among us.

6. My own thinking about the Psalms has taken place between the two quotes of Updike and Miranda that stand at the head of this book. Updike suggests that such religious language is "the words of the dead," the words that linger with power and authority after their speakers have gone. Indeed perhaps because we are "speech creatures," the most enduring thing about us is our serious speech to each other. So I take these psalmic words as "the voice of the dead," who may turn out to be the most living, present, and powerful ones among us (Hebrews 12:1). Updike's marvelous characterization of Rabbit comes when Rabbit is face-to-face with these powerful words that he cannot mock or dismiss

or trivialize, as he does almost everything else. That moment of candor is reinforced by Elie Wiesel's remarkable statement, "Poets exist so that the dead may vote." They do vote in the Psalms. They vote for faith. But in voting for faith they vote for candor, for pain, for passion — and finally for joy. Their persistent voting gives us a word that turns out to be the word of life.

On the other hand, at the far extreme, Miranda speaks out of a very different context. Whereas Updike speaks an artistic, literary reality, Miranda has almost no time for such aesthetics, but aims at the social reality. He brings to our work the hurt of the marginal and the critical tools of social analysis. I have not set out to do liberation theology, as Miranda might urge, for I have been committed to no goal but to hear the Psalms. But the psalm writers will not tolerate a faith in which human well-being is not honored. They are impatient with any God who thinks or acts otherwise. This Israelite insistence warns against any easy Christian spirituality. With force and regularity the questions of justice, righteousness, and equity are regularly brought to the throne, often to our surprise.

I am not sure that the offers of Updike and Miranda belong together. Updike's Rabbit would not think so, because passionate issues of justice are hardly in his purview. Too bad for Rabbit. Too bad for us, for Rabbit is a study about us and our affluent modernity. Perhaps that is why Rabbit at best is only at the very edge of this poetry. He cannot enter into it, claim it, affirm it, or be shaped by it. He cannot praise; he cannot cry out. And he is so much us. The Psalms are an invitation to Rabbit and all his clan to enter this world of dark discontinuity, for it is a world in which faithful address and answer make a transformative difference. That is why "we shall all be changed." The Psalms will not quit. They have not quit. And they keep inviting people like Rabbit into the wholeness that comes in embraced brokenness.

This new edition goes to press in the immediate wake of the disasters at the World Trade Center, the Pentagon, and the fields of Pennsylvania on September 11, 2001. These tragic events suggest how urgent the descent into disorientation is for the practice of faith.

Laugh at ministers all you want,
they have the words we need to hear,
the ones the dead have spoken.

Rabbit in John Updike, *Rabbit Is Rich*

It can surely be said that
the Psalter presents a struggle
of the just against the unjust.

José Porfirio Miranda, *Communism in the Bible*

1

The Psalms
and the
Seasons of Life

The Book of Psalms provides the most reliable theological, pastoral, and liturgical resource given us in the biblical tradition. In season and out of season, generation after generation, faithful women and men turn to the Psalms as a most helpful resource for conversation with God about things that matter most. The Psalms are helpful because they are a genuinely dialogical literature that expresses both sides of the conversation of faith. On the one hand, Israel's faithful speech addressed to God is the substance of the Psalms. The Psalms do this so fully and so well because they articulate the entire gamut of Israel's speech to God, from profound praise to the utterance of unspeakable anger and doubt. On the other hand, as Martin Luther understood so passionately, the Psalms are not only addressed to God. They are a voice of the gospel,

God's good word addressed to God's faithful people. In this literature the community of faith has heard and continues to hear the sovereign speech of God, who meets the community in its depths of need and in its heights of celebration. The Psalms draw our entire life under the rule of God, where everything may be submitted to the God of the gospel.

Psalm interpretation is at the present time beset by a curious reality. There is a devotional tradition of piety that finds the Psalms acutely attuned to the needs and possibilities of profound faith. (To be sure, some of that devotional literature is less than profound.) This tradition of Psalm usage tends to be precritical, and is relatively uncomplicated by any scholarly claims. There is also a well-established scholarly tradition of interpretation with a rather stable consensus. This tradition of interpretation tends to be critical, working beyond the naïveté of the devotional tradition, but sometimes being more erudite than insightful. These two traditions of interpretation proceed without much knowledge of, attention to, or impact on the other. The devotional tradition of piety is surely weakened by disregarding the perspectives and insights of scholarship. Conversely, the scholarly tradition of interpretation is frequently arid, because it lingers excessively on formal questions, with inability or reluctance to bring its insights and methods to substantive matters of exposition. This cleavage, of course, must not be overstated, for there are some contacts and overlaps among interpreters, but that contact is limited, modest, and too restrained.

What seems to be needed (and is here attempted) is a postcritical interpretation that lets the devotional and scholarly traditions support, inform, and correct each other, so that the formal gains of scholarly methods may enhance and strengthen, as well as criticize, the substance of genuine piety in its handling of the Psalms.

1. A long, faithful history of Psalms interpretation has developed in the service of the gospel that has been undisturbed even by the critical consensus. Today this understanding is embodied in personal piety that focuses on a few well-known and well-beloved Psalms, especially Psalms 23, 46, and 121. Such popular piety tends to be highly selective in the psalms used and frequently quite romantic in its understanding of them, so that the Psalms serve to assure, affirm, and strengthen faithful people. This selective (and romantic) tendency is reinforced by much liturgical practice in the church.

My criticism is nevertheless restrained, because the Psalms permit the faithful to enter at whatever level they are able – in ways primitive or sophisticated, limited or comprehensive, candid or guarded. The faithful of all "sorts and conditions," with varying skills and sensitivities, here find "the bread of life" as abiding nourishment. Any critical scholarship must respect that gift that is given and received in this literature, even if we do not understand the manifold ways in which that communication occurs.

2. Behind and before this popular contemporary usage, which continues the practice of many generations, we must also take account of another precritical use. Not only simple believers, but the great teachers of evangelical faith have also found the Psalms a peculiar resource for faith. They did so without the aid of much of our contemporary scholarship. Especially the great Reformers (Martin Luther and John Calvin) were driven in their evangelical passion and discernment precisely to the use and study of the Psalms.

These understandings of the Psalms are not only precious to us; they are decisive. We must not permit any of the gains of later critical scholarship to detract us from these claims. This, however, is not to suggest that the great reformers were "precritical." They did indeed practice and advance the best critical modes of study available to them, as we must.

We are not precritical people. We are heirs of a scholarly consensus that must not only be taken into account, but must be embraced as our teacher. In what follows, I shall try to deal with the Psalms, fully informed by the scholarly consensus, which may be summarized rather simply.

The main gains of Psalms scholarship have been made by the form-critical approach of Hermann Gunkel. It was his great insight that the forms of expression and modes of articulation in the Psalms can for the most part be understood in a few recurring patterns. (To be sure, not all psalms can be categorized in this way, and we need feel no special pressure to do so.) Moreover, these few typical modes of speech expressed certain characteristic gestures of faith, and they presumably reflect certain recurring life situations and/or liturgical practices. Thus what Gunkel saw is the convergence of modes of speech, religious claims, and social settings.

Based on Gunkel's insights concerning the form of these genres, our study of the Psalms may focus upon the typical, though details and specific developments in individual psalms must be noted. The rich details demonstrate the remarkable openness of the typical to various developments in the hands of various speakers.

The second major advance in Psalms study was made by Sigmund Mowinckel, a student of Gunkel. Mowinckel developed the hypothesis, which has attracted widespread and persistent scholarly attention, that these representative psalms are best understood in a single liturgical setting that dominated Israel's life. Mowinckel proposed that many of the psalms reflect the annual enthronement festival, enacted dramatically in the Jerusalem temple at New Year's time. In that festival, Yahweh, the God of Israel, is dramatically and liturgically re-enthroned for the new year, which is the renewal of creation and the guarantee of well-being. The

Davidic king in Jerusalem plays a major role in that ceremony, and of course, derives great political gain from the theological claims of the liturgy. Mowinckel found a way to comprehend many of the psalms in his remarkable hypothesis.

Scholarly reaction to his hypothesis is twofold. On the one hand, the hypothesis makes claims that are too broad and incorporates too many psalms of various kinds into a single action. And that action itself is premised on unsure comparisons, given the lack of clear Israelite evidence. Thus Psalms interpretation must be more pluralistic and diversified in order to allow the Psalms freedom to operate in many different aspects of Israel's life. On the other hand, for all its excessiveness, Mowinckel's hypothesis still occupies the center of the field and still provides the best governing hypothesis that we have. Thus we may permit it to inform our work as long as we treat it as provisional and are attentive to its temptation to be all-encompassing. It must be treated as a proposal and not as a conclusion. But given renewed interest in the liturgical character of the Psalms, Mowinckel's study offers a great many important insights for finding analogous uses in our own liturgical practice.

A third scholarly gain is the contribution of Claus Westermann. Following the form analysis of Gunkel and ignoring the liturgical hypothesis of Mowinckel, Westermann has urged that the complaint song is the basic form of psalmic expression, and that most other psalm forms are derived from or are responses to the complaint. He has shown that the complaint song expresses the basic moves of faith in God, ranging from deep alienation to profound trust, confidence, and gratitude. The major contribution of Westermann for our study is the discernment of a literary dynamic in the movement of the Psalms that corresponds to and gives voice to the dynamic of faith that we know in our experience with God.

4. This discussion will pursue a postcritical reading of the Psalms. That is, we shall try to take full account of the critical gains made by such scholars as Gunkel, Mowinckel, and Westermann, without betraying any of the precritical passion, naïveté, and insight of believing exposition. Specifically there is a close correspondence between the anatomy of the complaint song (which Westermann as a critical scholar has shown to be structurally central for the entire collection) and *the anatomy of the soul* (which Calvin related to his discernment and presentation of biblical faith). To pursue that close correspondence, we shall propose a movement and dynamic among the Psalms that suggests an interrelatedness, without seeking to impose a rigid scheme upon the poems, which must be honored, each in its own distinctiveness. Above all, we intend our interpretation to be belief-full, that is, in the service of the church's best, most responsible faith.

The following discussion is organized around

three quite general themes: psalms of *orientation,* psalms of *disorientation,* and psalms of *new orientation.* It is suggested that the psalms can be roughly grouped this way, and the flow of human life characteristically is located either in the actual experience of one of these settings or is in movement from one to another. By organizing our discussion in this way, we propose a correlation between the gains of critical study (especially Gunkel and Westermann) and the realities of human life (known to those who most use the Psalms in a life of prayer).

(a) Human life consists in satisfied seasons of well-being that evoke gratitude for the constancy of blessing. Matching this we will consider "psalms of orientation," which in a variety of ways articulate the joy, delight, goodness, coherence, and reliability of God, God's creation, and God's governing law.

(b) Human life consists in anguished seasons of hurt, alienation, suffering, and death. These evoke rage, resentment, self-pity, and hatred. Matching this, we will consider "psalms of disorientation," poems and speech-forms that match the season in its ragged, painful disarray. This speech, the complaint song, has a recognizable shape that permits the extravagance, hyperbole, and abrasiveness needed for the experience.

(c) Human life consists in turns of surprise when we are overwhelmed with the new gifts of God, when joy breaks through the despair. Where there has been only darkness, there is light. Corresponding to this surprise of the gospel, we will consider "psalms of new orientation," which speak boldly about a new gift from God, a fresh intrusion that makes all things new. These psalms affirm a sovereign God who puts humankind in a new situation. In this way, it is proposed that psalm forms correspond to seasons of human life and bring those seasons to speech. The move of the seasons is transformational and not developmental; that is, the move is never obvious, easy, or "natural." It is always in pain and surprise, and in each age it is thinkable that a different move might have been made.

But human life is not simply an articulation of a place in which we find ourselves. It is also a movement from one circumstance to another, changing and being changed, finding ourselves surprised by a new circumstance we did not expect, resistant to a new place, clinging desperately to the old circumstance. So we will suggest that the life of faith expressed in the Psalms is focused on the *two decisive moves of faith* that are always underway, by which we are regularly surprised and which we regularly resist.

One move we make is *out of a settled orientation into a season of disorientation.* This move is experienced partly as changed circumstance, but it is much more a personal awareness and acknowledgment of the changed circumstance. This may be an abrupt or a slowly dawning acknowledgment. It constitutes a

dismantling of the old, known world and a relinquishment of safe, reliable confidence in God's good
creation. The movement of dismantling includes a
rush of negativities, including rage, resentment,
guilt, shame, isolation, despair, hatred, and hostility.

It is that move that characterizes much of the
Psalms in the form of complaint and lament. The
complaint psalm is a painful, anguished articulation
of a move into disarray and dislocation. The complaint song is a candid, even if unwilling, embrace
of a new situation of chaos, now devoid of the
coherence that marks God's good creation. The
sphere of disorientation may be quite personal and
intimate, or it may be massive and public. Either
way, it is experienced as a personal end of the world,
or it would not generate such passionate poetry.

That dismantling move is a characteristically
Israelite move, one that evokes robust resistance
and one that does not doubt that even the experience of disorientation has to do with God and must
be vigorously addressed to God. For Christian faith
that characteristically Israelite embrace of and
articulation of disorientation is decisively embodied
in the crucifixion of Jesus. That event and memory
become the model for all "dying" that must be done
in faith. That is why some interpreters have found it
possible to say that the voice of anguish in the Book
of Psalms is indeed the voice of the Crucified One. I
do not go so far, and prefer to say the Christian use
of the Psalms is illuminated and required by the

crucifixion, so that in the use of the Psalms we are moving back and forth among reference to Jesus, the voice of the psalm itself, and our own experiences of dislocation, suffering, and death. There are, of course, important distinctions among complaint psalms. Thus *psalms of the innocent sufferer* more directly apply to Jesus than do the *psalms of penitence.* Nonetheless, taken as a whole, that dimension of the history of Jesus is a major point of contact for complaint psalms.

The other move we make is a move *from a context of disorientation to a new orientation,* surprised by a new gift from God, a new coherence made present to us just when we thought all was lost. This move entails a departure from the "pit" of chaos just when we had suspected we would never escape. It is a departure inexplicable to us, to be credited only to the intervention of God. This move of departure to new life includes a rush of positive responses, including delight, amazement, wonder, awe, gratitude, and thanksgiving.

The second move also characterizes many of the psalms, in the form of songs of thanksgiving and declarative hymns that tell a tale of a decisive time, an inversion, a reversal of fortune, rescue, deliverance, saving, liberation, healing. The hymnic psalm is a surprising, buoyant articulation of a move of the person or community into a new life-permitting and life-enhancing context where God's way and will surprisingly prevail. Such hymns are a joyous assertion that God's rule is known, visible, and effective just when we had lost hope.

That astonishing move is a characteristically Israelite move, one beyond reasonable expectation, one that evokes strident doxology because the new gift of life must be gladly and fully referred to God. For Christian faith, that characteristic Israelite articulation and reception of new orientation is decisively embodied in the resurrection of Jesus. That is why the church has found it appropriate to use such hymns with particular reference to Easter. This means that the use of these hymns and songs of thanksgiving moves back and forth among references to Jesus' new life, to the voice of Israel's glad affirmation, and to our own experience of new life surprisingly granted.

We may chart our way of relating the form of the Psalms to the realities of human experience:

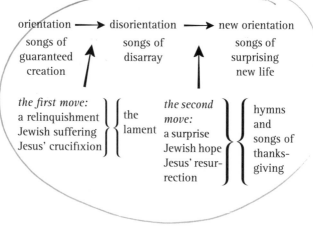

orientation ——→ disorientation ——→ new orientation

songs of guaranteed creation

songs of disarray

songs of surprising new life

the first move: a relinquishment Jewish suffering Jesus' crucifixion } { the lament

the second move: a surprise Jewish hope Jesus' resurrection } { hymns and songs of thanksgiving

The theological dimension of this proposal is to provide a connection among (a) focal moments of Christian faith (crucifixion and resurrection), (b) decisive inclinations of Israelite piety (suffering and hope), (c) psalmic expressions that are most recurrent (complaint and praise), and (d) seasons in our own life of dying and being raised. If the Psalms can be understood with these knowing sensitivities, our own use of them will have more depth and significance in the practice of both Jewish and Christian forms of biblical faith. In the last analysis, the Psalms have what power they have for us because we know life to be like that. In a society that engages in great denial and grows numb by avoidance and denial, it is important to recover and use these psalms that speak the truth about us – in terms of God's engagement with the world.

5. Before moving to the Psalms themselves, three preliminary comments need to be made.

(a) Clearly the move through this grid of orientation – disorientation – new orientation is not a once-for-all experience. In different ways, we frequently find ourselves in varying conditions in relation to God; but neither do I want to suggest any regularized movement of a cyclical kind. It is not difficult to see, however, that yesterday's new orientation becomes today's old orientation, which we take too much for granted and defend. John Goldingay has made the shrewd point that we not only slide from new orientation to old orientation, but also may find the same psalm serving to express either, depending on the context and intention of the speaker. Thus while I have offered a matrix, I do not want it taken too precisely, for life is in fact more spontaneous than that. I offer it simply as a way to suggest connections between life and speech, or as Paul Ricoeur puts it, between "limit experiences" and "limit expressions."

(b) The experience that these psalms interface may be of various kinds. Conventionally scholars have made a distinction between *communal* and *personal complaints*, and Westermann has correlated with that *songs of thanksgiving* and *hymns*. No doubt that is correct. But the point I make is that experientially, in terms of faith situation, the personal and public issues are all of a piece, and depending on our commitments, each may be experienced as the same threat or surprise of faith. I prefer to speak impressionistically, so that the actual experience may be of many different kinds, as long as it summons us to the same dynamics of faith.

(c) Such a grid in two movements reveals an understanding of life that is fundamentally alien to our culture. The dominant ideology of our culture is committed to continuity and success and to the avoidance of pain, hurt, and loss. The dominant culture is also resistant to genuine newness and real surprise. It is curious but true, that *surprise* is as unwelcome as is *loss*. And our culture is organized to prevent the experience of both.

This means that when we practice either move —
into *disorientation* or into *new orientation* — we
engage in a countercultural activity, which by some
will be perceived as subversive. Perhaps that is why
the *complaint psalms* have nearly dropped out of
usage. Where the worshiping community seriously
articulates these two moves, it affirms an understanding of reality that knows that if we try to keep
our lives we will lose them, and that when lost for
the gospel, we will be given life (Mark 8:35). Such
a practice of the Psalms cannot be taken for granted in our culture, but will be done only if there is
resolved intentionality to live life in a more excel-
lent way.

2

Psalms
of Orientation

The *psalms of orientation* were created, transmitted, valued, and relied upon by a community of faithful people. To these people, their faith was both important and satisfying. A beginning theological point for the Psalms are those psalms that express a confident, serene settlement of faith issues. Some things are settled and beyond doubt, so that one does not live and believe in the midst of overwhelming anxiety. Such a happy settlement of life's issues occurs because God is known to be reliable and trustworthy. This community has decided to trust in this particular God. Many of the psalms give expression to that happy settlement, to the reality that God is trustworthy and reliable, and to the decision to stake life on this particular God.

Here we will consider five representative types of

psalms that reflect well-oriented faith in a mood of equilibrium. These various poems are not easily assigned to any standard form. That is, they are statements that describe a happy, blessed state in which the speakers are grateful for and confident in the abiding, reliable gifts of life that are long-standing from time past and will endure for time to come. Life, as reflected in these psalms, is not troubled or threatened, but is seen as the well-ordered world intended by God. They approximate a "no surprise world" and consequently a world of "no fear." They do not report on an event, a happening, or an intrusion. Rather, they describe how things are and indeed always are. It will be clear that we are not following any strict form analysis, but are paying attention to the content and the mode of articulation.

These psalms in various ways are *expressions of creation faith*. They affirm that the world is a well-ordered, reliable, and life-giving system, because God has ordained it that way and continues to preside effectively over the process. At the same time, there is a profound trust in the daily working of that system and profound gratitude to God for making it so. Creation here is not a theory about how the world came to be. That is not how the Bible speaks about creation. It is rather an affirmation that God's faithfulness and goodness are experienced as generosity, continuity, and regularity. Life is experienced as protected space. Chaos is not present to us and is not permitted a hearing in this well-ordered world.

Foundational certainties are known to be operative in the world. The *nomos* (order) holds, and there is as yet no inkling of *anomie* (chaos). Experientially, of course, such certitudes have behind them previous awareness of disorientation, for that belongs to human experience. The process is continually dialectic. But formally, these psalms tend to disregard such previous experience and begin anew.

The function of this kind of psalm is theological, that is, to praise and thank God. But such a psalm also has a *social function* of importance. It is to articulate and maintain a "sacred canopy" under which the community of faith can live out its life with freedom from anxiety. That is, life is not simply a task to be achieved, an endless construction of a viable world made by effort and human ingenuity. There is a givenness to be relied on, guaranteed by none other than God. That givenness is here before us, stands over us, endures beyond us, and surrounds us behind and before. The poetic speech of the Psalms is our best language for such givenness, which is not initiated by us but waits for us. We experience a coherence that provides a context for our best living. Whenever we use these psalms, they continue to assure us of such a canopy of certainty — despite all the incongruities of life.

Notice that the Psalms not only point to such a protective reality; they evoke it, present it, keep it in place. This is a major gain of Sigmund Mowinckel's work on the creative power of public worship. Such worship is indeed "world-making." These psalms become a means whereby the creator is in fact creating the world. That perhaps is one meaning of the saying "God creates by Word." That creative word is spoken in these psalms in the liturgical process, and it is in the world of worship that Israel "re-experiences" and "redescribes" the safe world over which God presides.

Such high faith can be gladly affirmed, but it will also be better understood if we assess it critically. So it may be helpful to ask who experiences life this way and who wants most to make these kinds of assertions.

Such a satisfied and assured assertion of orderliness probably comes from the well-off, from the economically secure and the politically significant. That is, such religious conviction comes from those who experience life as good, generous, and reliable. This does not make these poems suspect, but it permits us to read them knowingly, for not everyone experiences life this way and can speak so boldly about it. Life is well-oriented only for some, and that characteristically at the expense of others. In these psalms we enter into the religious sensitivity and life experience of those who know life to have congruity, symmetry, and proportion. They are those whose "lines have fallen for me in pleasant places" (Ps 16:6). This means they have ended up with the best land, and so do not find it difficult to live a life of gratitude.

With such a suspicious possibility, we dare to suggest that creation faith, a sure sense of God's orderliness, is not always high and noble faith. Sometimes it is void of such pure motive and serves only to celebrate the status quo, the happy but inequitable way life is presently arranged. In using these psalms, we must be alert to the slippery ways creation faith easily becomes social conservatism, which basks in our own well-offness.

There are times when such psalms may be used freely. But there are certainly other times when such psalms must be used carefully or with a knowing qualification. For we know persons and communities whose experience of injustice and disorder deeply contradicts this faith. In any event, we must always ask whose interest is reflected and served by such psalms and by their use.

It follows that these psalms may not only serve as "sacred canopy" to permit communal life. They may also serve as *a form of social control.* Thus they may induct the young into a system of obedience and rewards, and so promote approved social conduct of a certain kind. They may also label the socially disapproved as the ones who violate God's creation. And they may be used to justify morally the view that those who do not prosper in the world are those who live outside the parameters and priorities of God's creation.

Creation faith is most usually articulated by the powerful people in society. It is the royal apparatus that experiences life as well-ordered. Creation faith subtly serves to grant self-approval, to warn dissenters, and to admonish children. In using these psalms, it will be important to watch for such partisan applications, which arise when God's creation is easily and unambiguously identified with our social experience of well-being and moral effectiveness.

Having said that, we may make one affirmation in another direction. The religious power of these psalms is considerable *for all sorts and conditions of people.* These psalms have been articulated by the socially successful, but their religious seriousness extends beyond the "successful." These same psalms provide a point of reference even for those who share in none of the present "goodies," but who cling in hope to the conviction that God's good intention for creation will finally triumph and there will be an equity and a sabbath for all God's creatures. It is for that reason that these psalms can be taken with an eschatological note, acknowledging that God's creation has not been fully completed, but this community waits with confidence. Such an eschatological note, I suggest, moves the psalm from its original social function of *social construction and maintenance* to this broader, more widespread use concerning *transformation and new creation.*

The Psalms speak of a healthy, oriented life that is anticipated, even if not yet experienced. There moves in these psalms a deep conviction that God's purpose for the world is resilient. That purpose will not yield until creation is brought to fullness. The Psalms assert that the creation finally is committed to and will serve the Creator. The Psalms thus are anticipatory of what surely will be. Strangely enough, they may serve as a point of criticism against the status quo, to assert that when the Creator's way comes to fruition, the inadequate present arrangements will be overcome. Thus the very psalms that may serve as *social control* may also function as a *social anticipation*, which becomes *social criticism*. But that requires that we become aware and intentional in our usage and the orientation that we articulate through them.

Songs of Creation

The most foundational experience of orientation is the daily experience of *life's regularities*, which are experienced as reliable, equitable, and generous. The community that composes and sings these psalms readily affirmed that this experience is ordained and sustained by God. A proper response is one of gratitude. The world is God's way of bestowing blessing upon us. Our times are ordered by God according to the seasons of the year, according to the seasons of life, according to the needs of the day. In all of these processes, we find ourselves to be safe and free; we know that out of no great religious insight, but because that is the way life comes to us. Consider some of the key examples in Psalms: 8, 33, 104, and 145.

Songs of Torah

When the creation is celebrated, it is acknowledged to be a well-ordered world. That order depends solely on God's power, faithfulness, and graciousness. That is why, in the face of the creation, Israel can only yield in praise. But there is more to it. The good order of *creation* is concretely experienced in Israel as the *torah*. The torah is understood not simply as Israelite moral values, but as God's will and purpose, ordained in the very structure of life. While the creation is sustained by God's faithfulness, it is also coherent and peaceable because of Israel's obedient attention to the way God has ordered life. Thus creation and torah are understood together, the torah articulating God's intention for Israel in the creation. See Psalms 1, 15, 19, 24, and 119.

Wisdom Psalms

Another expression of a well-oriented, reliable world is in the wisdom psalms. These tend to be didactic in tone and relatively amorphous in shape. They are best identified by their subject matter. Psalms 14 and 37 are good examples of this.

Occasions of Well-Being

All of the various psalms of orientation we have discussed thus far reflect a "peaceable kingdom." In all its parts, the "system" works, and the "system" refers to God's created order over which God presides in equity and faithfulness. The "system" also refers to a network of social relations, values, and expectations. On the basis of convincing firsthand experience the speaker in these psalms dares to postulate a correspondence between the way God orders the creations and the way in which society manages its choices. Everything is ordered and reliable. While the Psalms make that point theologically about God's governance *in heaven*, they also represent and reflect in *earthly* experience of the same order and reliability.

That orderliness and reliability is not a theoretical or abstract notion. It is known firsthand in the daily and seasonal experiences of life. Confidence in creation is based on the pattern of blessings that are known especially in the family, household, and tribe. The goodness of God is known here not by shattering intrusions but by quiet, unobtrusive sustenance. The regularity of creation is experienced in the predictable occurrences of birth, marriage, death, seedtime, and harvest. All these experiences testify to the Creator's regularity and reliability.

A number of psalms are occasional pieces that reflect and affirm God's goodness in the blessings of creation. In these, God is nowhere visible, but is discerned as the guarantor of the critical points through which life is affirmed and enhanced (see particularly Psalms 131, 133).

3

Psalms
of Disorientation

The problem with a hymnody that focuses on equilibrium, coherence, and symmetry (as in the psalms of orientation) is that it may deceive and cover over. Life is not like that. Life is also savagely marked by incoherence, a loss of balance, and unrelieved asymmetry. In our time – perhaps in any time – that needs no argument or documentation.

It is a curious fact that the church has, by and large, continued to sing songs of orientation in a world increasingly experienced as disoriented. That may be commendable. It could be that such relentlessness is an act of bold defiance in which these psalms of order and reliability are flung in the face of the disorder. In that way, they insist that nothing shall separate us from the love of God. Such a "mismatch" between our *life experience of disorientation* and our *faith speech of orientation* could be a great evangelical "nevertheless" (as in Habakkuk 3:18). Such a counter-statement insists that God does in any case govern, rule, and order, regardless of how the data seem to appear. And therefore, songs of torah, wisdom, creations, and retribution speak truly, even if the world is experienced as otherwise. It is possible that the church uses the psalms of orientation in this way.

But at best, this is only partly true. It is my judgment that this action of the church is less a defiance guided by faith and founded in the good news, and much more a frightened, numb denial and deception that does not want to acknowledge or experience the disorientation of life. The reason for such relentless affirmation of orientation seems to come, not from faith, but from the wishful optimism of our culture. Such a denial and cover-up, which I take it to be, is an odd inclination for passionate Bible users, given the large number of psalms that are songs of lament, protest, and complaint about the incoherence that is experienced in the world. At least it is clear that a church that goes on singing "happy songs" in the face of raw reality is doing something very different from what the Bible itself does.

I think that serious religious use of the complaint psalms has been minimal because we have believed that faith does not mean to acknowledge and embrace negativity. We have thought that acknowledgment of negativity was somehow an act of unfaith, as though the very speech about it conceded too much about God's "loss of control."

The point to be urged here is this: The use of

these "psalms of darkness" may be judged by the world to be *acts of unfaith and failure*, but for the trusting community, their use is *an act of bold faith*, albeit a transformed faith. It is an act of bold faith on the one hand, because it insists that the world must be experienced as it really is and not in some pretended way. On the other hand, it is bold because it insists that all such experiences of disorder are a proper subject for discourse with God. Nothing is out of bounds, nothing precluded or inappropriate. Everything properly belongs in this conversation of the heart. To withhold parts of life from that conversation is in fact to withhold part of life from the sovereignty of God. Thus these psalms make the important connection: everything must be *brought to speech*, and everything brought to speech must be *addressed to God*, who is the final reference for all of life.

But such a faith is indeed a *transformed* faith, one that does faith in a very different God, one who is present in, participating in, and attentive to the darkness, weakness, and displacement of life. The God assumed by and addressed in these does not *conform* (Romans 12:2). The community that uses these psalms of disorientation is not easily linked with civil religion, which goes "from strength to strength." It is, rather, faith in a very different God, one who is present in, participating in, and attentive to the darkness, weakness, and displacement of life. The God assumed by and addressed in these psalms is a God "of sorrows, and acquainted with grief." It is more appropriate to speak of this God in the categories of *fidelity* than of *immutability* (changelessness), and when fidelity displaces immutability, our notion of God's sovereignty is deeply changed. These psalms of disorientation are a profound contradiction to notions of an immutable God.

But the transformation concerns not only God. Life also is transformed. Now life is understood to be a pilgrimage or process through the darkness that belongs properly to humanness. While none would choose to be there, such seasons of life are not always experiences of failure for which guilt is to be assigned, but may be a placement in life for which the human person or community is not responsible and therefore not blamed. The presupposition and affirmation of these psalms is that precisely in such deathly places as presented in these psalms new life is given by God. We do not understand how that could be so or even why it is so. But we regularly learn and discern that there – more than anywhere else – newness that is not of our own making breaks upon us.

The linguistic function of these psalms is that the psalm may *evoke reality* for someone who has engaged in self-deception and still imagines and pretends life is well-ordered, when in fact it is not. The denial may be of a broken relationship, a lost job, a medical diagnosis, or whatever. The harsh and abrasive speech of a statement of disorientation may penetrate the deception and say, "No, this is how it really is." In such a case, *language leads experience*, so that the speaker speaks what is unknown and unexperienced until it is finally brought to speech. It is not this way until it is said to be this way.

It is no wonder that the church has intuitively avoided these psalms. They lead us into dangerous acknowledgment of how life really is. They lead us into the presence of God where everything is not polite and civil. They cause us to think unthinkable thoughts and utter unutterable words. Perhaps worst, they lead us away from the comfortable religious claims of "modernity" in which everything is managed and controlled. In our modern experience, but probably also in every successful and affluent culture, it is believed that enough power and knowledge can tame the terror and eliminate the darkness. A "religion of orientation" fundamentally operates on that basis. But our honest experience, both personal and public, attests to the resilience of the darkness, in spite of us. The remarkable thing about Israel is that it did not banish or deny the darkness from its religious enterprise. It embraces the darkness as the very stuff of new life. Indeed, Israel seems to know that new life is rooted nowhere else.

Whether this speech articulates, illuminates, or evokes experience, it does move the awareness and imagination of the speaker away from the life well-ordered into an arena of terror, raggedness, and hurt. In some sense this speech is a visceral release of the realities and imagination that have been censored, denied, or held in check by the dominant claims of society. For that reason, it does not surprise us that these psalms tend to hyperbole, vivid imagery, and statements that offend "proper" and "dignified" religious sensitivities. They are a means of *expressing* that tries to match experience, that also does not fit with religious sensitivity. That is, in "proper" religion *the expression should not be expressed.* But it is also the case that *these experiences should not be experienced.* They are speech "at the limit," speaking about experience "at the limit."

We may observe two factors that operate in the midst of this liberation of expression. First, the range of expressions employed here never escapes address to Yahweh. What is said to Yahweh may be scandalous and without redeeming social value; but these speakers are completely committed, and whatever must be said about the human situation must be said directly to Yahweh, who is Lord of the human experience and partner with us in it. That does not mean things are toned down. Yahweh does not have protected sensitivities. Yahweh is expected and presumed to receive the fullness of Israel's speech.

Second, though this speech is liberated and expansive, it tends to come to expression in rather consistent and rigorous forms. That is not because the speakers are dull and unimaginative and cannot think of a fresh way to speak; it is rather that the speech itself imposes a kind of recurring order in the disorientation, so that it has an orderliness of its own that is known and recognized in the community.

That form has been variously studied, first of all by Gunkel, and then refined in a most discerning way by Westermann. It will be understood that no single psalm follows exactly the ideal form, but the form provides a way of noticing how the psalm proceeds. That form has a dramatic movement that Westermann has usefully subsumed under two parts:

1. *Plea.* A complaint that God should correct a skewed situation.

(a) *Address to God.* The address tends to be intimate and personal. The complaint is not spoken by one who is a stranger to Yahweh, but one who has a long history of trustful interaction.

(b) *Complaint.* The purpose of the prayer is to characterize for God how desperate the situation is. While the situation may be variously one of sickness, isolation, imprisonment, or destruction, the imagery of the speech is most often about death. The rhetoric seeks to evoke from Yahweh an intrusive, transformative act. While it is not always the case, the complaint tends not only to describe a situation of urgent need, but to hold Yahweh accountable for it. The speaker intends to turn his problem into a problem for Yahweh, for it is Yahweh who is both able and responsible for doing something about it.

(c) *Petition.* On the basis of the complaint, the speaker makes a petition that asks God to act decisively. This element is perhaps the most intense because it is spoken as a bold imperative. No suggestion of either reticence or deference appears here. The speaker assumes some "rights against the throne" (Job 31:35-37), and so the urgency of the speech has a judicial quality. The speaker does, of course, ask for attentive compassion, but the speaker also insists on his rights. It is a plea for justice as much as mercy, with the suggestion that the unjust situation has arisen because of Yahweh's lack of attention.

(d) *Motivations.* Less crucial, but most interesting, is the inclination of the psalms to provide motivations to give God reason to act. Some of this is less than noble, but it is the speech of a desperate voice that has not time for being noble. At times the motivation comes peculiarly close to bargaining, bribing, or intimidating. But this also needs to be taken as a kind of parity assumed in the relationship. Among the motivations are these:

- The speaker is *innocent,* and so is entitled to help.
- The speaker is *guilty,* but repents and seeks forgiveness and restoration.
- The speaker recalls *God's goodness to an earlier generation,* which serves a precedent for God's goodness now. God should do once again what was done in the past.
- The speaker is *valued by God* as one who praises. If the speaker is permitted to die, the speaker will cease to praise, and the loss will be Yahweh's.
- The speaker finally goes beyond self and appeals

to Yahweh to consider *God's own power, prestige, and reputation.* Finally, the loss in death will not be to the speaker, but to Yahweh, who will be perceived as unable to care for his own.

Thus the motivation runs the spectrum from conventional covenantal concerns to a less "honorable" appeal to Yahweh's self-interest. The speaker has no time for theological niceties, but must secure action for his own well-being.

(e) *Imprecation.* It is clear that such speech tends to be regressive, that is, it moves into unguarded language that in most religious discourse is censored and precluded. Perhaps the most regressive element is the imprecation. This is the voice of resentment and vengeance that will not be satisfied until God retaliates against those who have done the wrong. While we may think this ignoble and unworthy, it demonstrates that in these psalms of disorientation, as life collapses, the old disciplines and safeguards also collapse. One speaks unguardedly about how it in fact is. The stunning fact is that Israel does not purge this unrestrained speech but regards it as genuinely faithful communication.

These five elements serve, on the one hand, to characterize how desperate is the need and place it at the throne of Yahweh, so that it is made unambiguously Yahweh's problem, and Yahweh must do something about it. God is treated as the responsibly governing One, when all the conventions of governance have failed.

2. *Praise.* When the psalm makes its next move, it is a surprising one. Things are different. Something has changed. We cannot ever know whether it is changed circumstance, or changed attitude, or something of both. But the speaker now speaks differently. Now the sense of urgency and desperation is replaced by joy, gratitude, and well-being. This movement from *plea* to *praise* is one of the most startling in all of Old Testament literature. The praise element tends to include three factors:

(a) *Assurance of being heard.* In the complaint discussed above, Yahweh is often accused of being absent, remote, unresponsive, not listening. Now that is changed. The speaker now is convinced that Yahweh has heard the petition. We may conclude that in stressful situations what we most yearn for is that we will be heard. That in itself is enough. Or alternatively, one must assume that if Yahweh has heard, he will act. It is not thinkable that God would hear and then not act. And therefore the crucial thing is Yahweh's hearing, from which everything else happily will follow.

(b) *Payment of vows.* Apparently, the speaker in time of trouble had vowed that if delivered he would keep a vow to give or pay something as an offering of thanksgiving and praise. Now in this moment joy, the speaker has not forgotten. And so this is an act of faithfulness, of keeping one's word.

Coming through the depth of the plea to the praise permits one to be generous. When life is freely given to one in "the pit," it evokes gratitude that motivates the full giving of offerings. Conversely, we may surmise, when one does not enter the pit honestly, then there can only be grudge and not gratitude, and likely no generous keeping of vows.

(c) *Doxology and praise.* The most important element of resolution is doxology and praise. The God who has been accused is now acknowledged as generous and faithful and saving. Now if one stands outside the poem, one may argue that this part of the psalm expresses the true character of God, worthy of praise. And the earlier accusation and protest are a misunderstanding and therefore unfair.

But if one enters into the poem and takes its movement as seriously reflecting the relationship between the two partners, then one must conclude that it is indeed the complaint that now moves Yahweh to act. And each part of the psalm must be taken "realistically" as reflective of a real moment in this relationship. Thus the sequence of *complaint–praise* is a necessary and legitimate way with God, each part in its own, appropriate time. But one moment is not less faithful than the other. In the full relationship, *the season of plea* must be taken as seriously as *the season of praise.*

(d) We may consider what happened to make the movement *from plea to praise* possible. Clearly there was some kind of action or transaction in the unspoken space of the poem between the two elements.

Thus, for example, in Psalm 13, something happened between verses 4 and 5. In Psalm 22, something happened between verses 21 and 22. It is possible that this was an "inward, spiritual" experience. More likely it was an outward, visible act by some member of the community, mediating the fresh move of Yahweh to the speaker. If this prayer takes place in a liturgical or quasi-liturgical setting, then the "in-between act" may be a gesture or a word by someone formally authorized to do so, for example, an elder, a priest, or some such functionary. Whatever it was must have had a profound emotional, as well as theological, impact on the complainer, for a whole new world of trust and gratitude is entered into in that moment.

The hypothesis of Joachim Begrich has been the most widely followed concerning this move. He proposed that an authorized speaker answered the plea in a standard "deliverance oracle." These speeches, now preserved in such texts as Jeremiah 30:10-11; Isaiah 41:8-13 and 43:1-7, originally stood at the in-between point in the psalm, but have now been separated into independent units in widely different parts of the Bible.

The deliverance oracle is a promise on God's part to be present with, to help, and to intervene on behalf of the petitioner. The recurring feature of such a speech is the sovereign "fear not" of Yahweh. And that speech – so goes the hypothesis – resolves the desperate situation and permits the

speaker to begin life anew in confidence and gratitude. It is argued that the "fear not" represents the
primal communication that touches the deepest
fears and angers and opens the most profound possibilities, when it is spoken by one who has consent
from us to change our world.

On purely literary grounds, Begrich's hypothesis
has much to commend it, because it shows the
detailed correlation of *complaint* (in the Psalms)
and *assurance* (in Isaiah 40–55). Begrich must argue
that texts now widely separated have this intimate
connection with each other. But, on the other hand,
the story of Hannah provides a narrative of a desperate petitioner who receives the word of assurance from a priest, Eli (1 Samuel 1:12-18).

The other factor that may illuminate Begrich's
hypothesis is an experiential one. We are speech
creatures. We do wait to be addressed. And when we
are decisively addressed by one with power and
credibility, it does indeed change our world.
Begrich's proposal permits us to proceed with some
awareness regarding the actual text.

What is clear in the text is a covenantal-
theological move from one part of the text to the
next. Beyond that, we are engaged in speculation.
We do not know concretely how this covenantal-
theological move was made. What we do know,
both from the *structure of the text* and *our own
experience*, is that grievance addressed to an
authorized partner does free us. That is the insight

behind Freud's theory of talk-therapy, that we do not move beyond the repressed memory unless we speak it out loud to one with authority who hears. In our culture we have understood that in terms of one-on-one therapy. We still have to learn that this is true socially and liturgically. These psalms provide important materials for that learning.

Personal Complaint Song

There is a great variety of psalms of disorientation. We begin our consideration of them with personal complaint psalms for two reasons. First, complaint psalms constitute a very considerable part of the collection. We will advance our argument if we see that complaint psalms are a quite standard and stylized way in which Israel articulated disorientation. Second, because the form is so clear in these, we will have easier access into the other psalms of disorientation when we see that the same issues are presented in a variety of different ways. The issue in all of these psalms is that something is amiss in the relationship, and it must be righted. This is not to suggest that the other psalms of disorientation are in any way derived from the personal complaint psalm, but that they participate in the same issues, which may be variously articulated.

These psalms are the voices of those who find their circumstance dangerously, and not just inconveniently, changed. And they do not like it. These are the speeches of caged men and women getting familiar with their new place, feeling the wall for a break, hunting in the dark for hidden weapons, testing the nerve and patience of those who have perpetrated the wrong. It is the function of these songs to enable, require, and legitimate the complete rejection of the old orientation. That old arrangement is seen, if not as fraud, at least as inadequate to the new circumstance. See, for example, Psalms 13, 35, and 86.

Communal Complaint Songs

It is probably easiest for us to resonate with personal psalms of complaint. Partly that is because they predominate in the Psalter and we are more familiar with them, even if we do not use them easily. But the other reason is that the category of the personal, even psychological, has become our mode of experiencing reality. We have, at the same time, experienced a loss of public awareness and public imagination. So while the personal complaints may parallel experiences of our own, the loss of public experience means we have little experiential counterpart to the communal complaint psalms. Given our privatistic inclination, we do not often think about public disasters as concerns for prayer life. If we do, we treat them as somehow a lesser item. We have nearly lost our capacity to think *theologically* about public issues and public problems. Even more, we have lost our capacity to practice prayer in relationship to public events.

The communal complaint psalms are statements about the religious dimension of public events of loss. They permit us to remember that we are indeed public citizens and creatures and have an immediate, direct, and personal stake in public events. The recovery of this mode of psalmic prayer may be important if we are to overcome our general religious abdication of public issues and the malaise of indifference and apathy that comes with the abdication. In a more general way, the public disasters of Israel were not unlike our own: war, drought, famine (see Job 5:19-22). Quite specifically, public energy in Israel's prayer was focused in the destruction of the temple in Jerusalem by the Babylonians. That focus is not hard to understand. The temple had come to be the point of reference for all of life. Its destruction thus meant the loss of a center, and a profound public disorientation, in which public meanings and values are nullified or at least severely placed in jeopardy.

The use of these psalms requires an imaginative identification of a "dynamic analogy," for the points of contact with our own experience are not so obvious and immediate as with the personal psalms. In using them, we may in a preliminary way think about comparable experiences and possibilities. The overriding symbolic threat in our time is the nuclear threat, which may be analogous to the threat against the temple. I do not suggest that the destruction of the Jerusalem temple is "objectively" of the same magnitude, but as a *functioning symbol*, the loss of Jerusalem is comparable to the loss of the whole "known world" threatened in our time.

Reflection on our own threat will enable us to enter into the emotive power of these psalms that ponder the loss of the temple. On a lesser scale, every threat of war, every piece of bad war news, tends to mobilize public imagination. Or in more centered, localized places, it can be done by a storm, a mining accident, or an epidemic. Or in another sense, our most vivid memories of public desolation came in the deaths of the Kennedys and Martin Luther King Jr. in the 1960s. Whether one is conservative or liberal, those events articulated and made inescapable a darkness and disorientation that could be covered up; but their power could not be denied. These psalms give us some access to those sensitivities. Romantic liberalism had imagined that such evil could not move against public institutions that seemed so sure. These psalms are deeply felt meditations on threats that now move against everything precious.

The communal complaints are not so numerous in the Psalter, but they are important for the nurture of responsible faith. The recovery of the personal complaint psalms is a great gain, but unless the communal complaints are set alongside them, the record of personal religion can serve only privatistic concerns – and that is no doubt a betrayal of biblical faith. To gain access to these psalms, therefore, we need to think through the public sense of loss and hurt and rage that we all have in common. This may include the various massacres carried out in the name of authorized governments, the endlessly exiled situation of Palestinians, the reality of worldwide oppression that is not "natural," but is caused by "the enemies" who trample on the public life and public future of large groups of people. It is stunning to think that prayer of this kind might indeed be the point of entry into the larger world of faith, where the Lord of the nations governs. Note especially Psalms 74, 79, and 137.

A "Second Opinion" on Disorientation

If one is alone in the world, disorientation may be handled by an uninterrupted monologue. Since there is only "us," we do all the talking. Our speech does not then evoke a response. Or if one believes that orientation and disorientation come in natural sequence, then the unsettlement may be viewed simply as a "passage" through which we must move. But in Israel, disorientation is not seen in either of these ways. It is not seen as a normal "passage," because real disorientation is a threat, and it evokes responses other than embrace. It is also not seen as a monologue, because in Israel life is always understood convenantally and dialogically.

Changed situations always concern both parties, God as much as Israel. Israel is expected to listen as much as speak. In the psalms we now consider, we have a "second opinion" about the disorientation, that is, how it looks to Yahweh. From these psalms we see that Yahweh views the matter in a very different way from the view in Israel we have discussed so far.

Disorientation is not viewed as a faceless situation nor as a passage, but as a *trouble in the relationship*. When God properly guarantees and when Israel properly responds in "trust and obedience," life will be well-oriented. Or at least that is the buoyant affirmation of the fully oriented. When orientation collapses, it is taken to mean that one of the two parties in the relationship has failed the other party. Trouble is lodged with one party or the other. Characteristically, each party assumes that the fault lies with the other.

In the psalms of personal and communal complaint, the speech is that of Israel addressed to Yahweh. On the whole, it is assumed that the trouble has happened because Yahweh has not adequately guaranteed a stable life. That is a conclusion that can easily be drawn if one trusts the affirmations of the songs of creation and torah. And so the speech urges Yahweh to act in a fresh way. We say, "on the whole," because that generalization is modified by one important factor. A third party in the skewed situation, in addition to Israel and Yahweh, is "the enemy." Sometimes disorientation comes, as in Psalm 137, through no fault of either Yahweh or Israel, but through the action of other human agents. But that does not alter the main dynamic of these prayers. Even when disorientation is caused by an enemy, the appeal is still to Yahweh. The appeal is not to the enemy that the enemy should desist, for that is a hopeless plea. The appeal is that Yahweh should intervene to right the situation and to punish the destabilizer. Sometimes Yahweh is blamed, and sometimes not. But when Yahweh is not blamed, he is nonetheless regarded as the only one who can intervene in a decisive and helpful way.

Not all the songs of disorientation are Israel's speech to Yahweh, and not all present Israel's view of reality. Not all songs of disorientation assume that the disorientation is Yahweh's fault, or Yahweh's to correct. There are a few psalms that put the shoe on the other foot, that assume that Yahweh speaks against Israel and calls Israel to repent in order that there may be restored covenant. Only in the most general way can these psalms be said to share any features of the genre of complaint. There are some complaints of Yahweh against Israel, but these are most likely to be in the prophetic litera- ture. Indeed, the prophetic lawsuit form does func- tion as Yahweh's complaint against Israel. Thus the psalms we consider here may seem to have more in common with prophetic than with psalmic litera- ture. We mention them here not because they are complaints of a common genre, but because they show another way of addressing the experience of disorientation (see Psalm 95).

In considering the complaint psalms, we have suggested the notion that the disorientation is laid at the door of Yahweh. In Psalms 50 and 81, a counterargument is made that the disorientation is due to Israel. Both judgments are biblical, and both need to be heard. The pivotal observation is that both arguments are made. Biblical faith must not be forced in one direction only. A sensitive pastoral use of the Psalms requires deciding which articulation is personally and theologically faithful in any given circumstance. The "second opinion" is not always the correct one. Sometimes the first opinion needs to be held to tenaciously.

4

Psalms of
New Orientation

I have tried to show that a major move of the Psalms is the move from an ordered, reliable life to an existence that somehow has run amok. The Psalms give expression to that new reality of disorientation, when everything in heaven and on earth seems skewed. We may believe that such psalms not only express what is already experienced. They also articulate and evoke the new situation of disorder so that it may be experienced. That is, it may not be fully experienced, embraced, acknowledged, unless and until it is brought to speech. We have seen that the experience of disorientation is experienced and expressed in many different ways. These different ways embody very different theological readings of reality, which cannot be explained by, understood through, or reduced to any single formulation. We have spent a major portion of our time and space on that reality in the Psalms because that is the part of the Psalter that has been most neglected in church use. In the present religious situation, it may be the part of the Psalter that is most helpful, because we live in a society of denial and cover-up, and these psalms provide a way for healing candor. It may also be so because we live in a society in which the disorientation is not only personal but also public. The "sacred canopy" is clearly in jeopardy, and that jeopardy must be dealt with as a religious issue.

But obviously the move into disorientation is not the only move made in the faith of Israel or in the literature of the Psalms. While the speaker may on occasion be left "in the Pit" (as in Psalm 88), that is not the characteristic case. Most frequently the Psalms stay with the experience to bring the speech to a second decisive move, from disorientation to new orientation. That is, the Psalms regularly bear witness to the surprising gift of new life just when none had been expected. That new orientation is not a return to the old stable orientation, for there is no such going back. The psalmists know that we can never go home again. Once there has been an exchange of real candor, as there is here between Yahweh and Israel, there is no return to the pre-candor situation.

Rather, the speaker and the community of faith are often surprised by grace, when there emerges in present life a new possibility that is inexplicable, neither derived nor extrapolated, but wrought by the inscrutable power and goodness of God. That newness cannot be explained, predicted, or programmed. We do not know how such a newness happens any more than we know how a dead person is raised to new life, how a leper is cleansed, or how a blind person can see (Luke 7:22). We do not know; nor do the speakers of these psalms. Since Israel cannot explain and refuses to speculate, it can do what it does best. It can tell, narrate, recite, testify, in amazement and gratitude, "lost in wonder, love, and praise."

Westermann has argued that the full form of the complaint psalm is the most basic rhetorical pattern in Israel's faith. That is because the full form constitutes a dramatic whole that moves from wretchedness to joy. It is important that the form, as currently understood, includes not only a statement of the *problem*. It also includes a statement of *resolution*, culminating in praise and thanksgiving. In the first instance, an act of praise and thanksgiving is a statement about *trouble resolved.* Thus the praise and thanksgiving forms in this case are not independent forms, but are partial forms. Initially every such statement has as its backdrop a situation of need and trouble. It is evident that these celebrative statements of resolution then break off and become independent speech forms, standing alone without their proper rhetorical forerunners. That is, we can have free-standing statements of new orientation for which God is gladly credited, but we will be helped to see that such statements of new orientation always have in their background statements of trouble.

The break point of the complaint form that turns *from plea to praise* is of course a literary phenomenon, but it does not illuminate how we receive the new experience of orientation. It simply gives expression to it. The question of how the move is made is not a literary, but a theological matter. Israel sings songs of new orientation because the God of Israel is the one who hears and answers expressions of disorientation and resolves experiences of disorientation. This good news reality must be fully appreciated for what follows. No amount of literary form or structure or habit will account for the new experience. Along with the *literary habit* that dominates these psalms comes the *theological experience* of the will and power to transform reality. All these prayers and songs speak of the intervening action of God to give life in a world where death seems to have the best and strongest way. The songs are not about the "natural" outcome of trouble, but about the decisive *transformation* made possible by this God who causes new life where none seems possible.

I must acknowledge two methodological factors. First, one must decide whether a psalm speaks of old orientation or new orientation. And second, it is evident that the psalms of new orientation offer a variety of solutions on a continuum of continuity and discontinuity. We shall see that the experiences and expressions of new orientation are rich and varied, for the newness of the treasure outdistances all the conventional modes of speech.

Personal Thanksgiving Songs

The most obvious song of new orientation is the thanksgiving song. The speaker is now on the other side of a lament or complaint. The occasion for the song is that the speaker has complained to God and God has acted in response to the complaint. The result of God's intervention is that the old issue has been overcome. The speech concerns a rescue, intervention, or inversion of a quite concrete situation of distress that is still fresh in the mind of the speaker. That is, these psalms tell stories of *going into the trouble* and *coming out of the trouble*. Compare these examples: Psalms 30, 34, 40, and 138.

Thanksgiving Songs of the Community

Since Hermann Gunkel it is conventional to regard songs of thanksgiving as belonging to the personal sphere. The counterpart in the public domain is the hymn. In general, this is a sound division. We may, however, identify a few public songs that are hymnic, but are songs of thanksgiving insofar as they speak about a specific answer to a specific cry concerning a specific trouble. Classification is not precise, but they are, in any case, songs of new orientation because they celebrate an act of God's power that has moved Israel's life out of a time of disorientation.

It is uncertain whether we may speak of a category of "communal thanksgiving," for the tendency is either to have the communal thanksgiving evolve into an individual song of thanksgiving (as in Psalm 66:13-20), or to become a general hymn of praise without reference to the particulars that belong to thanksgiving. Nonetheless, these psalms do suggest that on occasion the whole community had complained, the whole community had been saved, and therefore the whole community had given thanks. They reflect a public imagination capable of a troubled spirit, not so full of self, but able to reflect on its life in light of the majesty of God, a community forgiven and therefore ready to begin afresh. Look particularly at Psalms 65, 66, 124, and 129.

The Once and Future King

These are the songs of new orientation par excellence. They give public liturgical articulation to the "new kingship" of Yahweh, which has just now been established. It is likely that the enthronement songs are one version of *victory songs* that celebrate Yahweh's victory over Israel's enemies. In these psalms kingship is granted to Yahweh on the basis of the victory just won. Perhaps the primary example of

the victory song in the Old Testament is the Song of
the Sea (expanding on the Song of Miriam) in Exodus 15, which is reckoned as a very early liturgical
statement of the exodus from Egypt. It traces the
triumph of Yahweh in detail and likewise the defeat
of Pharaoh and the Egyptian gods. It is not our purpose to study that song in detail, but we may note
the following features.

1. Even though the psalm is historically specific,
it makes appeal to and use of the mythic vocabulary
and patterns of presentation that belong to the
ancient Near Eastern genre of victory song. The victory song is a strange mixture of the peculiarly historical experience of Israel and the common mode
of expression from the Near East.

2. The substance of the song is essentially narrative. It tells the story of the move of Israel by the
power of Yahweh from slavery in Egypt to settlement in the land. Israel's celebrative hymnody is
first of all a testimony to what has happened.

3. The conclusion in verse 18 is a formula of
enthronement, a conclusion to the narrative, a verdict upon the historical process just reviewed. This
verdict could stand alone in a liturgical formula
without the preliminary narrative, because the verdict is finally what counts. One might notice the
free-standing formulas of Christian worship, the
Doxology and the Gloria Patri, which are in fact victory claims that announce the triumphant authority
of Yahweh and deny the authority of other gods.

The victory-enthronement songs in the Psalter are probably derived in one way or another either from the exodus recital or from the Zion recital in which the exodus is retold in more mythic language.

The enthronement psalms, taken liturgically, eschatologically, politically, are an affirmation that all peoples – Israel and other peoples – as well as the whole created order, are accountable to God's governance. That is an enormous claim in a world bent on autonomy, threatened by normlessness. This rich metaphor of God's kingship may be considered theologically under at least five themes.

1. There is no doubt that the festal theme of Yahweh's enthronement draws heavily, if not decisively, on the *royal liturgy and ideology of the ancient Near East*. Thus the Israelite version of this common claim is that Yahweh is not simply an Israelite god, but the God to whom all the peoples are subject. Such a cosmic and universal claim precludes the reduction of Yahweh to a tribal, partisan, or sectarian God. As all peoples are accountable, so all peoples have a right to expect from this ruler a fair governance.

2. The theme of *kingship of God in Israel* also appeals to the old Moses-Sinai tradition. While these psalms are predominantly Zion-oriented, they allude to and play upon this covenant tradition, which is older than the temple tradition. That tradition asserts that from the earliest moment Israel's faith is articulated in a political metaphor. That

Yahweh is a royal power serves to destabilize every other royal power and to relativize every temptation to absolutize power. This kingship is a gift of freedom, for allegiance to this liberating God tells against every other political subservience (see Leviticus 25:42).

3. Because these songs probably belong to the Jerusalem liturgy, the kingship of Yahweh has intimate symbolic, political, and ideological connections to the kingship of the Davidic dynasty. Yahweh's kingship is politically significant as a way of *analyzing* all human exercise of power. But it is not only *critique*; it is also *authorization* for the peculiar vision of political authority held in Israel.

4. Christians will want to project these psalms toward the New Testament, for Jesus' central proclamation (Mark 1:14-15), articulated in many parables, concerns the kingdom and kingship of Yahweh. The New Testament does not proclaim the kingdom of Jesus, but the kingdom of *God*. That sweeping symbol comes to concrete expression not in a grand liturgical or political act, but in specific, powerful acts of compassion that transform (see Luke 7:22, which is an enactment of the commission of Luke 4:18-19). Jesus' ministry is a living out of the liturgical assertion of these psalms.

5. Our prayer life is a continued insistence on this metaphor. So Christians pray daily that God's kingdom come on earth (Matthew 6:10). Thus the liturgical act of these psalms of coronation is a sign

and expectation. Obviously, we are still short of implementation of the sign. So the liturgical decree of God's rule invites hope. And the hope of these psalms is important, for without this powerful transformative symbol, the pitiful regimes of the present age claim to be, and seem, absolute and eternal. Thus without this disruptive metaphor, oppressive regimes seem to be eternally guaranteed. It is not different on the American scene with our absolutizing of military capitalism. But we live in hope, because this metaphor keeps all present power arrangements provisional. They are all kept under scrutiny and judgement by this one who will finally govern.

Some of the clearest examples to read are: Psalms 29, 47, 93, 97, 98, 99, and 114.

Hymns of Praise

"Hymns of praise" would seem to be a very general classification. Indeed, there is a tendency to treat the term as a synonym for the Psalms. But in fact, it has a more precise reference. It characterizes a public (as distinct from personal or intimate) song that is sung with abandonment in praise to God for the character of God's person or the nature of God's creating and liberating actions. I am not sure whether, in the pattern of orientation – disorientation – new orientation that we have pursued, these psalms should all be placed at the very end of the process as surprising, glad statements of a new ordering of life, or whether they should be treated as the very deepest and established statement of the old orientation that is firm, settled, and nonnegotiable.

I place them here because the extravagant form of celebration does not seem jaded or fatigued with old orientation. It still seems bright, focused, and engaged, reflecting some sense of wonder and marvel at the gift of life recently given. On the other hand, some of the hymns are much more "descriptive" than "declarative." They have lost all specificity and seem only to affirm a well-ordered world. They not only have left behind the concreteness of the thanksgiving song, but perhaps also the vitality and enthusiasm of the new orientation. So it is the speech of newness on its way to being old, tired, established, and immovable. The descriptive hymns tend to be of the old orientation. More importantly, specific use might lead to the location of the hymn at one point or the other. But the *usage*, not the *content*, may determine its specific function in the community.

As a rule of thumb, we may assume that the more decisively declarative, the more the hymn speaks of new orientation; conversely, the descriptive hymn celebrates old orientation. We may also assume that the more the hymn focuses on historical liberation, the more likely it is about new orientation. Conversely, the more it focuses on creation, the more it is likely to attest to a long-established, enduring order – old orientation. We are in any case near to the closing of the circle by which the "new, new song" becomes an "old, old story."

Theologically, the hymn is a liturgical and unrestrained yielding of self and community to God. It is a disinterested, uncalculating ceding of life over to its pioneer and perfecter (Hebrews 12:2). It is an act of self-abandonment that embodies the first answer of the Westminster Catechism: "The chief end of man is to glorify God and enjoy him forever." The hymn is the way in which the faith community does its glorifying and enjoying in that specific destiny, as a foretaste of what is promised.

Some of the clearest examples to read are: Psalms 100, 103, 113, 117, 135, 146, 147, 148, 149, and 150.

5

Spirituality and
God's Justice

There can be no doubt that the Psalms are an important resource for spirituality and have been for countless generations. That is indeed why we continue to study them. These words have mediated the presence of God to persons and communities. The format for our presentations of the Psalms has assumed that authentic spirituality (that is, genuine communion with God) is never removed from the seasons, turns, and crises of life. So the modes of God's presence (and absence) and the quality of communion are very different in times of orientation and disorientation. What one says in conversation with God is deeply shaped by one's circumstance of orientation and disorientation. Relationship with God is not immune to the surprises and costs of our daily life.

Spirituality by itself, however, is an inadequate basis for reading the Psalms. For the most part, to place the Psalms in the domain of spirituality is a Christian approach, indeed, even an approach of a part of the Christian tradition. A very selected reading of the Psalms has been necessary to keep the Psalms within the confines of conventional spirituality. Taken by itself, the conventional perspective of spirituality does not fully take into account the decisively Israelite character of the Psalms. Throughout this study I have been aware of the startling assertion of José Miranda: "It can surely be said that the Psalter presents a struggle of the just against the unjust." To be sure, Miranda's judgment is also a partial perspective and does not include everything to be found in the Psalter. But it does point to something important that may draw us into the categories of Israelite faith.

The struggle of the oppressed against the unjust, when cast theologically, is the issue of *theodicy* (an examination of God's justice). These concluding comments explore the ways in which the notion of *spirituality* is treated in the Psalms in relation to the issue of *theodicy*. I do not want to schematize excessively, but I suggest that theodicy is a characteristically Israelite concern that may correct or discipline a Christian restriction of the Psalms to privatistic, romantic spirituality. That is, *communion with God* cannot be celebrated without attention to *the nature of the community*, both among human persons and with God. *Religious hungers* in Israel never preclude *justice questions*. Indeed, it is through the question of *justice* that *communion* is mediated:

> So if you are offering your gift at the altar, and there remember that your brother has something against you, leave your gift there before the altar and go; first be reconciled to your brother, and then come and offer your gift (Matthew 5:23-24).

My use of the category of theodicy has three dimensions. If spirituality is a concern for *communion with God*, theodicy is a concern for a *fair deal*. The juxtaposition of these themes, spirituality and theodicy, is to bring together *communion* and a *fair deal*. Such a juxtaposition is remarkable, because we do not normally worry about a fair deal when treating communion with God. But the psalmists do. And any spirituality we think we find in the Psalms that does not raise serious questions about theodicy has misunderstood the nature of psalmic faith.

The conventional idea of theodicy concerns God in relation to evil. If God is powerful and good, how can there be evil in the world? If the question is posed in this way, religion can offer no adequate logical response. Logically one must compromise either God's power or God's love, either saying that evil exists because God is not powerful enough to overrule it, or because God is not loving enough to use God's power in this way. To compromise in either direction is religiously inadequate and offers no satisfying response. Today the theological discussion seems to insist on holding on to God's love even at the risk of God's sovereign power. What faith offers is a sense of trust that is prepared to submit. That deep trust summons us to hard rethinking about the categories in which we do our reflection.

The characteristic way of handling theodicy in Old Testament scholarship, and in the theological enterprise more generally, is to see that the question becomes acute in Israel in the seventh–sixth centuries B.C.E., around the collapse of Jerusalem, temple, and dynasty. This approach sees the crisis growing out of a historical circumstance and brought to expression in a rich literary development. The historical experience of Israel suggests that God punishes capriciously, that the suffering is inappropriate to the disobedience; therefore God's justice is questioned. Specifically, the old theories (Deuteronomic and wisdom) that good people prosper and evil people suffer are reëxamined. Because the problem is so difficult, there is a rich array of literature that offers a series of imaginative probes around the question of God's justice, the best known of which is Job.

It cannot be denied that this is an important question. Such an approach, however, narrows the issue to a religious question about the character of God. Though the question grows out of historical experience and finds literary expression, it is treated as a theological question without any serious attention to other payoff systems of reward and punishment that are practiced in political and economic ways. But serious theodicy is always linked to social arrangements of access and benefit.

We already noted that genuine communion with God is never removed from the seasons, times, and crises of life. Or expressed another way, the question of theodicy is never a narrow religious question. It must be understood socially as a question about law, about the rule of law, about the reliability of the system of rewards and punishments. Theodicy then concerns the character of God as practiced in the system of values in a social matrix.

If we are to take seriously the question of theodicy in the Psalms, we must see that it cannot be reduced to or contained in a narrow question about God. Rather, theodicy is the rationale or legitimacy for the way in which society is ordered. It is a statement or agreement or compromise about how a society defines good and evil, right and wrong, power and powerlessness. The practical effect is that theodicy is a theory of power about who makes decisions and who obeys them, who administers and controls goods, who has access to them and on what terms. Or said another way, theodicy is an agreement about world-definition, about who gets to have a say, about who the authoritative interpreters are, and whose definitions and interpretations are "true" in this community. Theodicy is about the legitimacy of one's view of the world. The legitimacy of a worldview as "true" concerns theological matters, but it also includes all the power questions of law, economics, and politics. Reflections on theodicy, therefore, always spill over into the public dimensions of life.

Every theological settlement of the theodicy question is closely allied to a social scheme. If it is a statement about God, it inevitably includes a statement about the "truth" of God's agents – the priests, kings, prophets, theologians. In the language of Robert Merton, *theodicy* concerns the legitimacy of a rule of God about which there is assent and a general consensus. So long as the consensus holds, and no one dissents from the arrangement, then there appears to be no question of theodicy. It is correct that there is no *crisis* in theodicy, but that is a *consensus* about theodicy all the same. Theodicy operates in times of equilibrium as well as in times of crisis, but it is often hidden. We are agreed, and so we instruct our children, that this is the order to be honored and obeyed. We objectify and reify that order in a positivistic way, so that there is no room outside the consensus from which to mount a criticism. Obviously such an accepted theodicy is a form of social control and conformity. There is no crisis, but there is a theodicy, conventionally legitimated by the rule of God.

A *theodicy of consensus* is operative in every stable society. In our western society, we have had a consensus of justice about how to organize marriage and the respective roles of men and women. Because there was consensus and the arrangement was properly legitimated, it was experienced as just. Now that a criticism has been mounted (through feminist voices), we begin to see that the arrangement was not always just, and so the conventional theodicy is in crisis. And it is easy to see how this becomes a God-question, because in conventional industrial society, the family arrangement was not only perceived as workable and just, but as legitimate, blessed, and approved by God as the right way to order social life. Now it is clear that if God continues to legitimate that social arrangement as the proper and only form of life, then God's justice is much in question. The shift from *a consensus about theodicy* to *a crisis in theodicy* can be identified in every liberation movement that questions the old settled arrangements.

A crisis occurs in a societal scheme of theodicy when some members of the community (perhaps a class or social group) conclude that the agreed settlement is inequitable and not to be honored. There may then be a harsh end to docility and the articulation of vigorous dissent. Because the challenged theodicy includes both a *doctrine of God* and *a social system of authority*, the challenge may take one of two forms:

1. It may be concluded that the entire arrangement, theological as well as social, is to be rejected,

because the legitimating God is in collusion with the human exploiters; and the collusion is so deep and unjust that the whole system must be rejected. Seen in that radical way, the Exodus-Conquest tradition is a protest against an established Egyptian theodicy. Israel rejects not only Egyptian civil authority, but also the Egyptian gods. The Egyptian gods are seen to be so enmeshed with the unjust social system that it must all be rejected. And in rejecting the entire social system, Israel introduced a new social system (torah) and a new God (see Joshua 24:14-15; Judges 5:8). That is, Israel adopted an entirely different *scheme of theodicy*, erected a new rule in the form of torah, and the entire movement was marked by egalitarianism.

2. On the other hand, it may be concluded that the human system is corrupt and unfair, but the legitimating God is reliable. Then a distinction can be made, so that by appeal to and in the name of the still trusted God, the old system is rejected as unjust and disobedient to the will of God, who is just. This could be the case in ancient Israel in the rejection of the old greedy judges and the establishment of the monarchy as a new social system (1 Samuel 8:1-5), the northern rejection of the exploitative dynasty of the south (1 Kings 12:16), or the purging of the monarchy around the boy king, Joash (2 Kings 11:17-20). In each case, the justice of Yahweh is not questioned, but only the social systems that claim Yahweh's legitimacy. In

each case, the human agent is rejected and the divine legitimator is retained.

In our day, there are also feminist theologians who radically criticize the social system, but who in the very name of God propose a new social system, that is, a new functioning theodicy. In the Old Testament, both modes are present: sometimes appeal is made to Yahweh against the system; sometimes appeal is also made against God, as in Job.

From this social analysis of theodicy, the conclusions of the ethicist Jon P. Gunnemann follow. Social *revolution* of a serious and sustained kind is in fact an act of *theodicy*. The precondition of revolution is a theodicy that declares that some should be happy and others should be miserable because they lack access to the blessings. Revolution happens when the theodicy is perceived as unacceptably unjust. That is, every stable society assigns persons to places in life that are relatively powerful or powerless. That arrangement is necessary to maintain equilibrium; it feeds on a functionalist sociology. Serious revolution, as Gunnemann characterizes it, is not simply an effort to transfer goods and rights of special benefits from one group to another. It is rather a rejection of the ground rules, a challenge to the paradigm that makes this arrangement possible. It is an attempt to change the rules of access and distribution so that a more just and humane practice can be initiated. What appears as *order* to some will be experienced by other as *exploitation.* What appears as *subversion* on the part of the old regime may be perceived as *quest for justice* on the part of those who undertake the change. What the old regime regards as *sacred rule* is seen by others to be *legitimated lawlessness*, but nonetheless lawlessness, *anomie.* And so, drastic alternatives are required that change the rules of the game. That surely is what the Exodus is about in Israel and every appeal that is subsequently made to that tradition.

Our understanding of theodicy, therefore, includes the following dimensions:

• Theodicy is *a religious crisis* about the character of God.
• Theodicy is *a social crisis* that doubts the social settlement of goods and power and assaults the legitimation of that settlement.
• Theodicy is *revolutionary action* that seeks to displace the rules of the game.

Miranda's comment merits our attention because it affirms to us that psalmic spirituality is preoccupied with the question of theodicy, though the question may be put in any of these three dimensions. This conviction may help us understand and appreciate why it is that the Psalms frequently and pervasively speak about the "righteous" and the "wicked," about the *righteousness of God* and the trustworthy *rule of God.* What emerges from this dominant vocabulary is that Israel is not interested in spirituality or communion with a God that tries to deny or obscure the important issue of theodicy. An unjust relation with God is no relation at all. A skewed communion is not a communion worth having. The psalms crave for and mediate communion with God, but Israel insists that communion must be honest, open to criticism, and capable of transformation. These are the prayers of a people with a deep memory of liberation and a profound hope for a new kingdom. This people is not prepared to submit again to the yoke of injustice as they had done in Egypt (see Galatians 5:1). The psalms suggest that Israel is nearly incapable of an address to God that does not confront the issue of justice and righteousness.

The issue may be handled in two ways, as we have suggested above. On the one hand, in a few texts *God, along with the social system*, seems to be rejected. In these harsh statements, the critique is made not only of "the enemy" but also of God who has been unjust or absent. In those extreme cases, the issue of theodicy is acute and painful, because in fact the psalmist has no other court of appeal and so must come back in appeal to the very one who has been accused. In these cases, the prayer questions whether God is just, without even speaking of the social system God legitimates.

On the other hand, more often, appeal is made to God, *against the system.* In those cases God is assumed to be just and faithful, but it is "the enemy" who has perverted God's way and so must be judged. In that case, the appeal to God makes sense, for it is against one who has violated God's known will.

The *vocabulary* of justice and righteousness, of wickedness and innocence, as well as the *forms* of accusation, complaint, and thanksgiving, prepare us for a sustained reflection on the theme.

We have seen that the psalms of orientation tend to be consolidating, stability-enhancing, and inclined to urge conformity. These psalms reflect a theodicy that is accepted and celebrated without question. They reflect society "in a state of homeostatic equilibrium." They mean to affirm the order, to generate new allegiance to the order, to give the order more power and authority, and to inculcate the young into it. This may be an act of good faith, but such a voice also benefits from the present arrangement.

Even if there is not a social crisis, therefore, the social arrangement is no less a theodicy. It means to affirm and insist that the order holds, and the way to life is to submit to this unquestioned order.

In this religion God is indeed confessed as equitable and just. And for these people the present arrangement, blessed by God, does yield an abundant life. These psalms, as Mowinckel understood, not only celebrate order, but generate it.

When these psalms are used, that is their function. And so a spirituality that focuses on these psalms is not likely to be disinterested. It celebrates the coherence of life and the justice of God because that is how they are experienced. This is life fully oriented, finding the current rules on earth and in heaven adequate. Such a spirituality intends to keep life fully oriented.

Gunnemann, quoting Johnson, uses our terminology. Such a theodicy may "define violence as action that deliberately or unintentionally disorientates the behavior of others." Then revolution is treated as a "disease."

From this perspective, we may observe three dimensions of disorientation that are commonly treated as pathological:

- It is pathological to challenge the present order of economic and political power.
- It is pathological to suggest that God may be unjust.
- It is pathological to speak, as some of these psalms do, in a voice of disorientation.

The psalms of disorientation occur and make sense to us when the consensus about theodicy has collapsed and there is a crisis in the ordering of life. We have explored a variety of directions in which these psalms may develop. The fact that they take many different postures is not difficult to understand. It is because in a season of disarray one does not know how best to move. Three strategies are evident, following the three foci that Westermann has discerned:

1. They are a *yearning for retaliation* against the unjust enemy who has made life so disoriented.

2. They are *assaults on Yahweh* as the legitimator of the theodicy, because on some occasions not only is the social system awry, but the God who legitimates the system seems to have failed as well. Not only the order, but the *guarantor of order* is in question. This speech is incredibly bold, because the speaker has nowhere to address the speech except back to the same agent.

3. Occasionally the speech of disorientation has a yearning for a *return to the orientation* and is able to accept the fault, as in "the seven psalms" (Psalms 6, 32, 38, 51, 102, 130, 143). But even in these, the righteousness of God is discerned as something other than it had been perceived. The righteousness of God becomes a point of appeal that lies outside the standard explanations.

In any case, this speech is revolutionary in that it violates the conventions of the fully ordered world. But Gunnemann observes that such speeches of violence

> . . . may have a meaning that *does* orient the behavior of others, namely, the members of a revolutionary party, or of a marginal group, or of a social class; or it may represent the attempt on the part of such groups to bring into being a new system of meaning for the society as a whole. Revolutionary violence disorients only those who remain committed to the established order or those against whom the violence is directed.

I find Gunnemann most helpful, though I have to some extent changed the terms of his analysis. In the Psalms we do not have violent acts, but only violent speech. And the violent speech is often directed against Yahweh, who is perceived on occasion as the perpetrator of violence. What is important in this analysis is that the aim is to "bring into being a new system of meaning for the society as a whole" (Gunnemann). But a new system of meaning will not come without abrasion, and that is what these psalms offer. A disruptive break with the *theodicy of consensus* is a prerequisite to a new *theodicy of justice.*

The psalms of new orientation celebrate a new settlement of the issue of theodicy. The crisis is past, and there is again a stable paradigm for social life. Revolutions do not so readily succeed, but in the life of the liturgy, one advances the hunch and hopes that this result will come. The liturgical event is a foretaste of the real settlement. So these psalms of new orientation speak about the new state of things when life is whole and well-ordered, when the system is just and God is known to be righteous and just. It is for that reason that the starting point for such psalms may be either the songs of personal thanksgiving or the enthronement psalms. In the former, one has had an intimate and undeniable *experience of new order.* In the latter, one gives public articulation to the *establishment of a new governance* that has moved decisively against the idols that are the agents of unjust order. What is clear in these psalms is that this is not a return to the old theodicy. There is here no knuckling under to the old regime, the old God. There is rather a celebration of the coming of God, who now establishes a new rule. In the language of the sociologist, this is the establishment of a reliable order. In the parallel language of Israel, it is the governance or the torah that matters. And these psalms reveal a happy readiness to live according to the order that now replaces the old order, which had been so distorted that it was in fact a way of disorder.

With this analysis of theodicy, we may now return to the matter of the Psalms as resources for spirituality. The Psalms are resources for spirituality; but any psalmic spirituality that denies or avoids the parallel issue of theodicy misses the point. That is, the spirituality of the Psalms is shaped, defined, and characterized in specific historical, experiential categories and shuns universals. Such recognition does not require a fresh exegesis of each psalm, so much as hermeneutical insistence about the categories through which the psalms are to be understood. The Psalms have been central to a spirituality that is individualistic, otherworldly, or centers on a quest for meaning. But if I read them rightly, the Psalms characteristically subordinate "meaning" to "justice." The Psalms regularly insist upon equity, power, and freedom enough to live one's life humanely. The Psalms may not be taken out of such a context of community concerns.

When we pray these Psalms, in community or in

private, we are surrounded by a cloud of witnesses who count on our prayers. Those witnesses include first of all the Israelites who cried out against Pharaoh and other oppressors. But the cloud of witnesses includes all those who hope for justice and liberation. This does not detract from the conviction that God is powerful Spirit. It does not reduce the Psalms to political documents. It rather insists that our spirituality must answer to the God who is present where the questions of justice and order, transformation and equilibrium are paramount. We dare not be positivists about our spirituality, as though we live in a world in which all issues are settled. The spirituality of the Psalms assumes that the world is called to question in this conversation with God. That permits and requires that our conversation with God be vigorous, candid, and daring.

God assumes different roles in these conversations. At times God is the guarantor of the old equilibrium. At other times God is a harbinger of the new justice to be established. At times also God is in the disorientation, being sovereign in ways that do not strike us as adequate. We might wish for a God removed from such a dynamic, for a spirituality not so inclined to conflict. But the Psalms reject such a way with God as false to our daily life, and false to the memories of this people, who know they do not belong to the Egyptian empire, but who hope for a new equilibrium in a kingdom of justice and righteousness. On this the Psalter insists passionately, vigorously, and boldly.

Bibliography

Brueggemann, Walter. *Abiding Astonishment: Psalms, Modernity, and the Making of History.* Literary Currents in Biblical Interpretation. Louisville: Westminster John Knox Press, 1991.

——. *Israel's Praise: Doxology against Idolatry and Ideology.* Philadelphia: Fortress Press, 1988.

——. *The Message of the Psalms: A Theological Commentary.* Minneapolis: Augsburg, 1984.

——. *Praying the Psalms.* Winona, Minn.: St. Mary's, 1982.

——. *The Psalms and the Life of Faith.* Edited by Patrick D. Miller. Minneapolis: Fortress Press, 1995.

——. *Theology of the Old Testament: Testimony, Dispute, Advocacy.* Minneapolis: Fortress Press, 1997.

Gerstenberger, Erhard S. *Psalms, Part 1; with an Introduction to Cultic Poetry.* Forms of the Old Testament Literature 14. Grand Rapids: Eerdmans, 1988.

——. *Psalms, Part 2; and Lamentations.* Forms of

the Old Testament Literature 15. Grand Rapids: Eerdmans, 2001.

Gunkel, Hermann. *An Introduction to the Psalms.* Completed by Joachim Begrich. Translated by J. D. Nogalski. Mercer Library of Biblical Studies. Macon, Ga.: Mercer Univ. Press, 1998.

Holladay, William L. *The Psalms through Three Thousand Years: Prayerbook of a Cloud of Witnesses.* Minneapolis: Fortress Press, 1993.

Kraus, Hans-Joachim. *Theology of the Psalms.* Translated by K. Crim. Continental Commentaries. Minneapolis: Augsburg, 1986.

Mays, James Luther. *The Lord Reigns: A Theological Handbook to the Psalms.* Louisville: Westminster John Knox, 1994.

Miller, Patrick D. *Interpreting the Psalms.* Philadelphia: Fortress Press, 1986.

———. *They Cried to the Lord: The Form and Theology of Biblical Prayer.* Minneapolis: Fortress Press, 1994.

Mowinckel, Sigmund. *The Psalms in Israel's Worship.* Translated by D. R. Ap-Thomas. 2 vols. in 1. Nashville: Abingdon, 1962.

Reid, Stephen Breck. *Listening In: A Multicultural Reading of the Psalms.* Nashville: Abingdon, 1997.

Westermann, Claus. *Praise and Lament in the Psalms.* Translated by K. R. Crim and R. N. Soulen. Atlanta: John Knox, 1981.